Practical Applications

of the

Shotokan Kata Jion and Jiin

by Carsten Schmitt

3rd Dan Shotokan

4th Dan World Combat Association

AF140257

Warning

The methods described and demonstrated in this book are potentially dangerous and must not be attempted by anyone unless under supervision of a qualified instructor. Any persons attempting any of the activities described in this book do so entirely at their own risk. All readers are encouraged to be aware of, and adhere to, all appropriate laws related to self-defense. Some of the techniques and methods described in the book require high levels of skill and physical fitness. A physician has to be consulted before practicing them.

Note

The author, publishers and distributors of this book do not accept any responsibility for any use or misuse of the containing information and related prosecution or official proceedings against anyone or any loss, injury or damages caused hereby.

Carsten Schmitt

Practical Applications

of the

Shotokan Kata Jion and Jiin

Bibliografische Information der Deutschen Nationalbibliothek:
Die Deutsche Nationalbibliothek verzeichnet diese Publikation in der
Deutschen Nationalbibliografie; detaillierte bibliografische Daten
sind im Internet über http://dnb.dnb.de abrufbar.

Illustration: **Carsten Schmitt, Ilka Schmitt (Fotos)**
Übersetzung: **Carsten Schmitt**
weitere Mitwirkende: **Jens Gödecke (Darstellung)**

Herstellung und Verlag: BoD – Books on Demand, Norderstedt
ISBN: 978-3-7357-2485-4

Contents

Practical applications of Shotokan Kata Jion and Jiin

Introduction

This analysis was prepared to support the 4th Dan grading of Carsten Schmitt with Sensei Iain Abernethy of the World Combat Association in November 2012. It contains description of practical applications of the two Shotokan Karate kata Jion and Jiin, shows how the two kata are related from an application point of view and brings them into a combative context. Since there are many inter-pretations of single techniques this work can not cover all. However it can be seen as comprehensive since it deals with all sequences in both kata and explains the system, strategies and tactics behind them. It should enable the reader to built on it and to develop his / her own approach to the two kata. The appendix includes illustra-tions of the two forms and a drill for training purposes.

Acknowledgements

Special thanks to Ilka, my beloved wife, for taking the photographs and for the patience she has with her Karate-maniac. I know it is not easy with me. Also I want to thank my training partner Jens Gödecke for his support, his fighting spirit and continuous work in the dojo. The dojo is the home of a Karateka and so I thank Leo Stibitz and all the other mates from our dojo in Idar-Oberstein for giving me a home. I should not forget to pass thanks to the man who brought me to the wonderful art of Karate Sensei Martin Hartung. I would not be where I am without him. We have established a firm network dealing with practical kata applications and everything around our martial art. I want to thank all people in that network for the inspiring conversations and the time we share with each other. My friends Nicolas Hofele and Axel Siebert have to be mentioned in the first place. I also found the lessons live or on video from Patrick McCarthy, Kit Sien Tjong, Gilbert Gruss, Volker Schwinn and Werner Lind very inspiring and made use of it in my training. Last but not least I want to thank Sensei Iain Abernethy for supporting my progress, for his guidance and for giving me the opportunity to do the 4th Dan grading under his supervision.

Kata Bunkai and Self Protection

It's not very likely that well educated and behaving people are used to getting involved in fights. Usually they are taught to avoid them and are not seeking for them. This is also the most important rule for self defense: The fight which has not started can not cause any damage. Therefore everyone dealing with self defense should learn how to avoid fights before they learn how to end them. This should also be part of our martial arts training if we want to make use of it for self protection.

Kata can help if you get beyond this point. As soon as a confrontation becomes violent it will be a very chaotic affair which you have to go through avoiding injuries. When you are under attack usually the body functions work different and adrenaline takes over. It is no longer the smooth and almost clean environment a martial artist is used from the dojo. If you train kata in a way it was designed then it can help you creating awareness for such situations and having a plan to escape. It delivers strategies, tactics and techniques to incapacitate aggressive opponents.

In order to train kata in that way you have to understand that real fights are not like competition. There is no mutual agreement to start and stop the fight enforced by rules and a referee. Real fights don't end when it gets painful or dangerous. Distances are completely different than in competition where you often interrupt attacks to get back to a more defensive posture. Also you will hardly find blocks in real fights because they simply don't work. Blocks can work from a distance when an attack can be anticipated, but not when you are surprised or the attack comes for example from behind. Real fights are getting very quickly close and are often ended very fast by a blow to the head. They also can get very easily to the ground which is a very dangerous position to be, especially if the opponent is not alone.

Kata provides a template how you may act under attack. As a fighting system on its own it gives you a guideline which techniques you can use to address attacks by untrained and violent opponents. It was developed for civilian self protection and not to fight trained and skillful warriors. In order to make use of the benefits kata has to offer you need to analyse, understand, train and drill the applications that you create the skills to automatically use them under bad, insecure and unpredictable circumstances. Therefore you also need to consider practicing the fighting skills from the kata in the dojo with incompliant partners. This will teach you that not everything works at any time with any opponent and that what can go wrong is likely to go wrong. Even then you need to be ready to react and find another solution to escape or to end the fight. Kata can help you to switch between alternatives if you understand them and have trained its applications accordingly.

Shotokan Kata Jion and Jiin

This document deals with the Kata Jion and Jiin from the Shotokan Karate Style. There origin is not completely clear, but both kata are seen as typical for Shotokan since they are usually not taught in other styles. It is often mentioned in literature that the two kata belong to a group of three (Jion, Jiin and Jitte) and that they are related. But apart from the same starting syllable "Ji", the same starting position and the common powerful techniques there is hardly anything else mentioned. From a practical point of view this analysis will show that there are lots of similarities between the two kata. They are based on the same strategies and tactics and provide answers for similar situations with variations of defensive themes. Therefore it is also easy to mix the applications of the two kata for example in training drills.

General Kata Principles

Each kata works based on some common principles which you need to understand to make effective practical use of them:

1) Kata is a holistic fighting system:

Each kata is a stand-alone self-protection system which contains a strategic guideline, tactics and combative technical tools. It trains the mindset and physical fitness. Having that in mind is crucial to understand the applications and fighting themes around a specific kata.

2) Kata is combat:

Every kata movement is designed for use in combat. They need to be able to end a confrontation immediately. That's why a lock or a hold is not a primary fighting technique. A kata has to be performed with fighting spirit, at full concentration and with utmost precision in order to be able to use the applications in combat.

3) Kata shows a way through the chaos of combat:

Practicing kata means learning a game plan for fighting which can help to overcome the chaotic circumstances of a fight. It needs to be trained with "unwilling" partners that it can work in real situations. The adrenaline rush can make your techniques imprecise and weak. Also you can easily be surprised and trapped when under adrenaline because your awareness and perception does not work normal. Therefore it is better to work with the adrenaline rush and not against it.

4) Actions and reactions are not choreographed:

If you practice kata in the way described above none of their techniques can work relying on what an opponent does. You need to take over control, create and maintain dominance. Keep the opponent busy. Try to enforce predictable responses from the opponent. You should exploit them if possible and also consider pre-emptive actions in order to get control over the opponent and the fight as much as possible.

5) Kata techniques need to be performed effectively and with furiousness:

"Strike to disrupt, disrupt to strike" like Kane and Wilder state in their book "The way of kata". Strikes should hit anatomical weak points. They need to be practiced with full power, at high speed and with high precision. Nerve strikes should not be tried for its own sake but can create additional benefit.

6) Kata provides a variety of techniques and applications:

There can be more than one effective application for each kata movement. Actions at every range need to be considered. All parts of a movement have a meaning and need to be examined in order to understand why and how they are supposed to work. Stances and angles are vital elements of this. A stance is a snapshot of a movement and teaches how to change position and shift weight in order to perform applications as effective as possible. Angles in a kata show where you have to be positioned in relation to the opponent in order to make the application work. For example techniques to the rear usually means that you should be behind the opponent when executing them.

If a kata is understood based on the principles above you need to train it accordingly in a way that you can benefit as much as possible from it and make use of it for self defense.

Strategy and Tactics from Jion and Jiin

In my view there is a strategic goal which both kata have in common. If you make a target with one of your hands at the opponent's head it is easier to hit it. This is something the starting position of both kata indicate. The open left hand grabs the head, the right hand punches to it. Alternatively it can be something else than a punch - a grab to the throat or a neck breaker - which will be described later. I believe that this is a strategic offensive theme of both kata because it will end a confrontation immediately and it is a method to overcome the limited ability to hit when you are under adrenaline. It is simply easier to hit a target when you have contact to it and don't need to rely on your visual perception alone. The fact that it is shown at the beginning of both kata indicates the importance the creator of the kata has seen in it. The kata contain concepts to avoid or counter grabbing the head or a punch to it. Then it tries to get the attacker's limbs out of the way in order to get behind the opponent. For that the limbs should be moved over the head (jodan height) or in front of the body (gedan or chudan height). If that does not work many of the techniques also work from the front. All techniques can be used in different close ranges, from punching distance or the clinch.

Applications from Jion and Jiin

Now it will be looked at the applications of both kata. It will not be exactly in the order of the kata because the analysis deals with the parts of the kata which have similar applications in order to show their relation. Several themes will be described which can be linked together in various orders. In the grading syllabus there are also drills out of different applications included which follows this idea.

For simplicity common terminology is used the Shotokan book reader is familiar with to describe techniques and moves. The formal description does not necessary match with the function. For example "Age Uke" means a forearm upper block but can be a forearm smash to the head.

1) Attacking the head

The first part of this analysis deals with the introductory posture and its strategic and tactical interpretation as well as it's alternative applications. There are basically four themes described which deal with attacks to the head.

Picture 1: Introductory posture

As explained above this posture indicates that the head should be held with one hand (right handed people usually do it with the left hand as shown in the kata) and the other hand comes into action – either by a punch, a throat grab or a neck breaker. All variations need to be executed in a way that they end the fight immediately.

Picture 1.1: Punch

Hold the head with the left and punch to the chin or throat with the right.

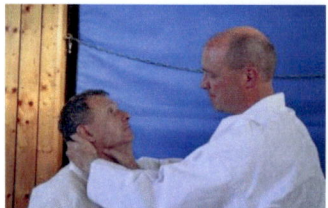

Picture 1.2: Throat grab

Hold the head with the left and grab the throat with the right.

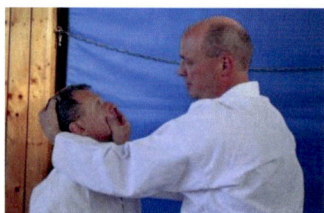

Picture 1.3: Chin grab

Hold the head with the left and grab the chin with the right. Be careful that the opponent can't bite your hand or thumb. Then start turning the head.

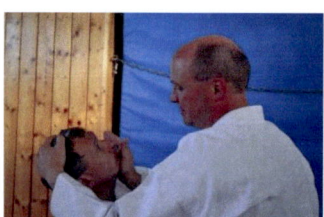

Picture 1.3.1: Turn the head

Picture 1.3.2: Neck crank

Picture 1.3.3: Finishing technique at the floor

A fourth alternative for the beginning posture of the kata and the following backward move is to see it as a clinch around the neck of the opponent. You can hit him in the neck at the rear base of the skull (gall bladder 22) in order to shock and distract him. Then turn his head around and try to get his back in front of you. This will give you an advantage because you will be in a position to dominate the opponent.

Picture 1.4: Clinch with both hands in the neck of the opponent

Picture 1.4.1: Hit to the neck

Jion and Jiin now step back in Zenkutsu Dachi and do a „double block" Uchi Uke and Gedan Barai. This brings the opponent down by a neck crank before he can be finished off. Jion does the Uchi Uke with the right hand and Gedan Barai with the left. Jiin does it vice versa. That shows that the following should work on both sides.

Picture 1.4.2: Zenkutsu Dachi „double block" Uchi Uke / Gedan Barai

Picture 1.4.3: Grab with the right hand to the ear, chin or eyes

Picture 1.4.4: Turn the head and get into the back of the opponent

2) Protecting the head

The initial move also shows a defensive theme against an attack to the head. It can be used against a grab to the head in order to prevent the opponent from setting a target or controlling the head. Or it can be a protection against a straight punch or a swinging blow. Another way to see this move is to use it in order to break the throat grab or the clinch and escape from it. Also here the fact that the beginning moves in both kata change sides indicates that it should work on both sides.

Picture 2: First backward move from kata Jion (left) and Jiin (right)

The following two pictures show that the Uchi Uke can protect the head so that the opponent cannot grab it or punch it. In a variation the protecting arm can be held in a way that the hand touches the back head and make a triangle with the elbow pointing in direction to the breast of the attacker. Then it is no longer a strictly formal Uchi Uke but very similar and effective since the triangle is very stable and makes it difficult for the attacker to reach the head.

Picture 2.1: Uchi Uke protects the head, Gedan Barai controls the other arm

If the head is hold with two arms the attacker might push it down in order to kick it with the knee or to strike you in the neck like shown in picture 1.4.1. It's necessary to get out of this situation and by pushing one arm up (like with Uchi Uke) and the other down (like with Gedan Barai) the grip can be broken.

Picture 2.2: Clinch by attacker

Picture 2.2.1: Escape by striking with left arm to the elbow, down into Geda Barai and with right arm up into Uchi Uke (Jion version)

Picture 2.2.2: Same move with other arms like in Jiin

The same move works if your throat is grabbed by the attacker like shown in picture 1.2. Then you push the choking hand away with Gedan Barai and the hand holding the head with Uchi Uke. Also against the chin hold of picture 1.3 it will work. This gets you in a position to move on with the concepts of both kata.

3) Moving arms over the head

This chapter is about a way to move one of the attacker's arms over your head to the side that you get out of his attacking direction and behind him. As stated before this does not always work and therefore it will also be discussed about what to do if the attempt fails. Both kata have Kakiwake Uke which are followed by a kick and strikes. The following series of pictures describe how this should work to get behind the attacker and what the following kick and strikes are supposed to do.

Picture 3: Kakiwake Uke

The Kakiwake Uke can be executed from the end position of the prior chapter. Also the intuitive cover shown in the next picture can be the starting point. This cover is very natural because as soon as a punch is launched to your head and you see it coming you will raise your arms to cover the head.

Picture 3.1: Intuitive cover of the head

If the attacking arm is deflected to the top the arms can be crossed under it.

Picture 3.1.1: Crossing arms under the attacking arm

The arm is moved over the head and the defender might make a step to the side in order to get behind the attacker.

Picture 3.1.2: Behind the attacker

Then the kick to the knee has to follow either from the side as shown in the next picture or even completely from behind if the defender has moved that far behind (see picture 3.1.5).

Picture 3.1.3: Mae Geri Kick to the knee

In Jion the next techniques are three punches (Oi Zuki, Gyaku Zuki, Oi Zuki). This should show that the attacker should be hit with whatever punch is possible. Since most people are right handed the emphasis is on the right hand. That's why the kata shows two out of three punches with the right hand.

Picture 3.1.4: Three punches (Sanbon Zuki) out of Jion

Instead of the third punch Jiin shows an Uchi Uke and Gedan Barai like in the initial move. The punches can end the confrontation by knocking the opponent out and the double technique from Jiin can be applied from behind in order to hold him with one arm up and one arm down.

Picture 3.1.5: Alternative version from Jiin

There is no guarantee that you can come behind the attacker with the move. In a chaotic fight this might not work and then there needs to be a way to defend from the front. That is certainly not the first choice but one needs to be able to react in that case as well. The Kakiwake Uke can also work from the front when the shoulder of the opponent close to the defender will be pulled and the other one will be pushed. At the same time the defender steps out of the attacking direction. This is shown in both kata since they do the Kakiwake Uke in a 45° angle. The pulling arm can cover at the same time and the pushing arm holds the other arm away from the defender that it cannot reach him.

Picture 3.2: Hold shoulders of attacker and push / pull

What follows then is the same like described before. There is a kick to the knee (or to the groin) and then the following punches.

Picture 3.2.1: Kick to the knee

Picture 3.2.2: Jion version with three following punches (Sanbon Zuki)

The hold from Jiin replacing the third punch can also be done from the front. There Uchi Uke arm goes under the armpit of the attacker and the Gedan Barai arm will hold the other arm of the opponent. The fight can then be ended for example with a head butt.

Picture 3.2.3: Hold from front and head butt

4) Moving below the attacking arm to counter

Instead of bringing the arm over the head you can move below the arm and attack low for example the groin. Both kata offer the Manji Uke for that concept – in opposite directions and often with a turn. The high Uchi Uke holds the attacking arm up opening the way for the Gedan Barai to strike low.

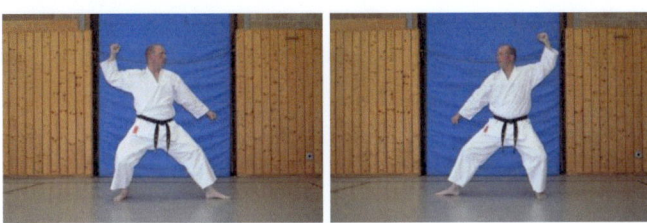

Picture 4: Manji Uke (to both sides at several points in both kata)

Also here it can start with a intuitive cover of the head.

Picture 4.1: Intuitive cover of the head

Then the attacking arm will be grabbed and hold up while the defender's free arm attacks low with a strike to the groin. Here the turn (known from the kata form) to the attacker is important in order to get to the target.

Picture 4.3: Holding the attacking arm up and strike low

Jion suggests at different points some alternatives to continue from there. First you can slide behind the attacker and punch him to the ribs or get the arm around his neck for a choke.

Picture 4.4.1: Side slide with punch to the ribs (alternative 1 from Jion)

Picture 4.4.2: Side slide with choke from behind (alternative 2 from Jion)

At a later point in the form there is an arm breaker or another choke from behind following the Manji Gamae. This choke is reinforced by the second arm supporting the one around the neck.

Picture 4.4.3: Side slide, lift up and strike the elbow from below (alternative 3 from Jion)

Picture 4.4.4: Side slide and reinforced choke from behind (alternative 4 from Jion)

In Jiin Age Uke and Oi Zuki follows the two Manji Gamae at the beginning. This would be another possibility to continue after the strike to the groin. In Chapter 6 it will be looked at the Age Uke and Oi Zuki or Gyaku Zuki combination in more detail.

If the strike to the groin or the following techniques for any reason cannot be applied Jion shows in the last sequence a way to react on this. Instead of using a Gedan Barai move to the groin or moving behind the attacker after it you can also directly punch to the head with a Mae Te Zuki (straight punch) or a Tettsui Uchi (side hammer fist strike).

Picture 4.5.1: Mae Te Zuki (direct punch to the head)

Picture 4.5.2: Tettsui Uchi (side hammer fist to the head)

5) Throws instead

There are some similar move like the Tettsui Uchi from the end of Jion in Jiin. Those moves have spins at the beginning or at least a side turn. That's why I think that Jiin would rather see them as throws than as strikes. In order to make the throws work you need to get one leg behind the attackers legs and either punch or pull him over your lead leg. The following sequences demonstrate this idea. As usual it is possible to do that on both sides, but here only one is shown.

Picture 5.1: Bring the lead leg behind the opponent and strike with the hammer fist (Tettsui Uchi) to push him over the leg

Picture 5.1.1: Instead of striking over the opponent's arm you can hold his lead arm up and push on the breast to throw

Picture 5.2: Hold the attacker at the neck and pull him over your lead leg to let him fall

Keep in mind that after a throw you either need to apply a finishing technique or even better make use of the attackers imbalance and lost orientation to escape. With those throws there is a risk that you also go to the floor. In that case make sure that you get in control of the situation and either get up quickly again to escape or get on the attacker in a position where you can control and dominate him.

6) Forearm upper block or slam (Age Uke)

Age Uke is often explained as an upper block to protect the head. In a combative context I would rather see it as an attacking technique either to the head or to a limb which is already under control. It can also be a move to get or hold a limb out of the way of a following strike. Like mentioned before Jiin lets the Age Uke follow directly after the Manji Gamae. This can either be a technique to control the arm which was lifted up or to attack this arm or the head. Then a punch - depending on the distance - either Oi Zuki or Gyaku Zuki will be next.

The Age Uke can also help to counter a grip to your collar which the opponent might apply to stop your Manji Uke attack. With this grip he maybe wants to stop you from turning into him for the groin strike. The grip can be done with one hand or with both if he makes it to free the hand from your uplifting hand.

Picture 6.1: Grip from the front with one or both hands

If you are hold like this you need to escape and counter because the attacker can easily launch his next attack. In order to make the following easier to read the first Age Uke with the left side in Jion will be described. It will work the same way on the other side. First you should step to the right side in order to get out of the attack direction of the opponent. At the same time the left arm strikes the inner elbow of the attackers left arm and your right arm points towards the opponent's face. This is to avoid a head butt since the head will move forward due to the elbow strike (predictive response).

Picture 6.2: Step to the right, left arm striking elbow, right arm to the head

Then the left arms does the Age Uke as a slam to the head while the right hand goes back to the attackers left hand to keep control over it.

Picture 6.3: Age Uke with left to the head, right hand controls attacker's left hand at the collar

Now either a Gyaku Zuki or an Oi Zuki can follow. Jion shows both alternatives (two Gyaku Zuki and then an Oi Zuki) while Jiin shows Oi Zuki only after the Age Uke. From a practical point of view this simply depends on the distance you need to bridge to impact the opponent. If he tries to get away after the Age Uke you probably need an Oi Zuki, if the Gyaku Zuki will not reach him.

Picture 6.3.1: Gyaku Zuki from the stance

Picture 6.3.2: Oi Zuki with a step forward

There is an alternative way where you need to react fast enough to get the attacker's arm before it can grab your collar. If the arm which should grab your collar is pushed away then you can also use the Age Uke to control this arm and lift it up in order to strike the opponent with Gyaku Zuki or Oi Zuki.

Picture 6.4: Arm pushed away with right, Age Uke with left and then Zuki will follow

7) Move limbs in front of body (Gedan or Chudan)

Before we have predominantly brought the attacking arm over the head to the side in order to get out of the attacking direction and behind the opponent. Probably that's the most intuitive and preferred way of both kata. I see two reasons for this:

i) The head is the preferred target of an attacker. Therefore you raise the hands up to protect it. And since they are already up it is the shortest and most intuitive way to bring the attacking arm over the head to the side.

ii) Both kata have Kakiwake Uke at several points which shows that the creator of the kata recognizes the importance of this theme.

However the limbs can also be directed low (gedan or chudan height) in front of your body to the side in order to accomplish the same. The Gedan Barai moves at the beginning of several straight lanes in both kata stand for this theme.

Ideally you come in position to the attacker like shown in picture 7.1. Pull the attacker's arm down and then pull it to the side with your other arm in order to break his balance and open the way for a counter attack.

Picture 7.1: Getting „behind" the attacker by directing the attacking arm low in front of your body

Even more effective would be applying the Gedan Barai as an arm lock by pulling the attacking arm straight while pushing it's elbow down.

Picture 7.2: Taking the arm at the elbow with your other arm and pulling to the side in order to open a way for the counter attack

Jion shows the Tate Uchi with Kiba Dachi stance in its first straight lane as a counter attack. This should be directed to the best possible target to reach – either the head or the body (e.g. the ribs).

Picture 7.3: Tate Uchi with Kiba Dachi

If unfortunately you do not come out of the attacking direction you need to instantly move on with the counter attack.

Picture 7.4: Arm pulled down but still in attacking direction of opponent

Picture 7.5: Tate Uchi to head or body to follow immediately

Instead of the Tate Uchi from Jion a Shuto Uchi can be applied as shown in Jiin. Here the target is for sure the head. It can be hit from the front to any point in the face or even the throat or from behind to the neck.

Picture 7.6: Shuto Uchi strike to the head

The second application Jion has from this position is the Hiza Geri (knee kick) with the following Otoshi Uke (hammer fist strike from above).

Picture 7.7: Hiza Geri and Otoshi Uke

8) Hold from front with both hands

The Age Uke chapter 6 dealt already with a situation where the defender is in a front hold either with one or two hands to the collar. This could be a reaction against the Manji Gamae move but it can also occur for many other reasons. Often holding someone with both hands should control him and help pushing him somewhere where he cannot easily escape – for example in a corner. Jion deals with that hold and whatever may follow in a complete lane after the second Manji Gamae with the arm breaking Jodan Morote Uke.

With a hard strike to the elbows the head of the attacker will move forward (predictive response). Be careful not to get hit by the head, grab around the body or neck, pull down and kick with the knee to the groin, belly or chest . Push the bent body down and strike to the head. Then move back and push the opponent to the ground.

Picture 8.1: Beginning of Jion lane with double down strike to the elbows

Picture 8.2: Hold around body or neck, pull and kick with the knee (Hiza Geri)

Picture 8.2.1: Push the body down and punch (Gedan Juji Uke)

Picture 8.2.2: Step back and push the opponent to the ground (double Gedan Barai)

Instead of the knee kick Jion shows another way. As soon as the strike to the elbows has been done and the attacker's head comes towards the defender the fists can be pushed to it in order to stop it. Then the head can be hold and hit with a straight strike.

Picture 8.3: Both fist strike to the head (double Uchi Uke in kata Jion form)

Picture 8.3.1: Grab the head and strike (Jodan Juji Uke)

If you are controlled with both hands at your collar there can be several ways to be attacked. In case you cannot escape with the techniques described above you need to be prepared to fight those attacks. Jion offers three ways to do that:

If the opponent launches an attack from the top. You can deflect it with an Age Uke and counter with an Uraken (backhand strike) to the head. This can be repeated until the opponent let you go or has been knocked out.

Picture 8.4: Age Uke defense and Uraken counter attack

An attack from the side can be parried with what Shotokan practitioners would call the preparing move for a Soto Uke or Ura Zuki. At the same moment the other arm pushes forward with a Zuki to the attacker's head, shoulder or chest in order to hinder him from moving forward and attack.

Picture 8.5: Hitting shoulder or breast while protecting the head from the side

A low attack like an Ura Zuki or a grab to the collar can be answered with a down block striking the attacking arm. The other arm does an Ura Zuki to counter the attack.

Picture 8.6: Down block with Ura Zuki

All three techniques have a certain order in the kata but can be varied in whatever order is necessary.

9) Hold from front with one hand

The next sequence in Jion deals with a way to escape being seized from the front with one hand. As described above this is a critical situation because the attacker can feel where you are and it will be much easier for him to hit. As an immediate reaction Jion proposes to strike the elbow of the holding arm. This brings the attacker down and his head moving forward (predictive response). Then the same hand goes back to strike the head with Uchi Uke. With a step forward the head is seized and with a step backward the opponent should be thrown. After this the attacker can be finished off with a Zuki while he is falling or already on the floor.

Picture 9.1: Preparing move for Uchi Uke as strike to the elbow

Picture 9.2: Uchi Uke (backhand strike) to the forward coming head

Picture 9.3: Grab holding arm with Uchi Uke arm and push forward in Oi Zuki

Picture 9.4: Seizing the head and stepping back to throw

Picture 9.5: Zuki to the head

10) Jiin end

The final sequence of Jiin contains many themes already discussed but however brought in a bit different context. It begins for example with a sequence similar to what followed the Kakiwake Ukes. The block motion from picture 28 in appendix 2 can be seen as a push to the shoulder of an attacker who holds you with one hand at the collar. The kata shows the push in a 45° angle in order to step out of the attacking direction. It can be done from below or above the attacking arm. Then a Gyaku Zuki and Oi Zuki to the head, a Mae Geri kick to the knee inner and another Gyaku Zuki to the head follow.

Picture 10.1: Two ways of pushing against the attacker's shoulder (from below or above)

Picture 10.2: Gyaku Zuki hit to the head

Picture 10.3: Oi Zuki hit to the head

Picture 10.4: Mae Geri kick to the knee inner (kicking leg going back again)

Picture 10.5: Gyaku Zuki hit to the head

Then a similar sequence like described in chapter 9 is next. The Gyaku Zuki arm strikes the still holding arm at the elbow followed by an Uchi Uke backhand strike to the head. Instead of throwing the defender gets behind the attacker with changing hands like indicated in the kata by the turn and changing Uchi Uke / Gedan Barai (pictures 33 and 34 of appendix 2). The Gedan Barai takes the holding hand in an arm bar and the Uchi Uke holds the head from behind. Then both arms can be fixed on the back which opens for Zukis to the head or neck from behind in order to finish the fight.

Picture 10.6: Strike to the elbow

Picture 10.7: Uchi Uke to the head

Picture 10.8: Gedan Barai to lock the right arm and get behind attacker while Uchi Uke seizes the head

Picture 10.9: Seizing both arms from behind and guiding down (double Gedan Barai from kata)

Picture 10.10: Bringing both arms to the back (double Uchi Uke)

Picture 10.11: Choku Zuki to the rear head or the neck

It was mentioned earlier that many techniques and combinations can work from behind and the front. In this case there is an application for the double Uchi Uke which can work as a wrist lock from the front. After the last Gyaku Zuki (Picture 10.5) the hand hold at your collar can be turned in a wrist lock while the other hand strikes the attacker's neck. Then the head will be pulled to the rear while the wrist lock is held. The following Zukis to the head will end the fight.

Picture 10.5.1: Wrist lock, strike to the neck and pulling the head back (double Uchi Uke from kata)

Picture 10.5.2: Hits to the head

Conclusion

I hope my analysis showed why the two kata Jion and Jiin are related from a practical point of view. Beside similar techniques they
share the same underlying strategies and tactics and deal with the
same issues. As mentioned there are for sure many additional inter-
pretations of the techniques with high practical value. It is impossi-
ble to discuss them all in an analysis like that. However the analysis
is supposed to be comprehensive in the sense that it shows practical
applications for the complete kata and explains them as fighting sys-
tems. All single themes discussed above can be mixed in training
drills. The grading syllabus in appendix 4 shows some of them and
gives guidelines how to train and make practical use of the two
Shotokan kata Jion and Jiin.

Appendix 1: Jion Form

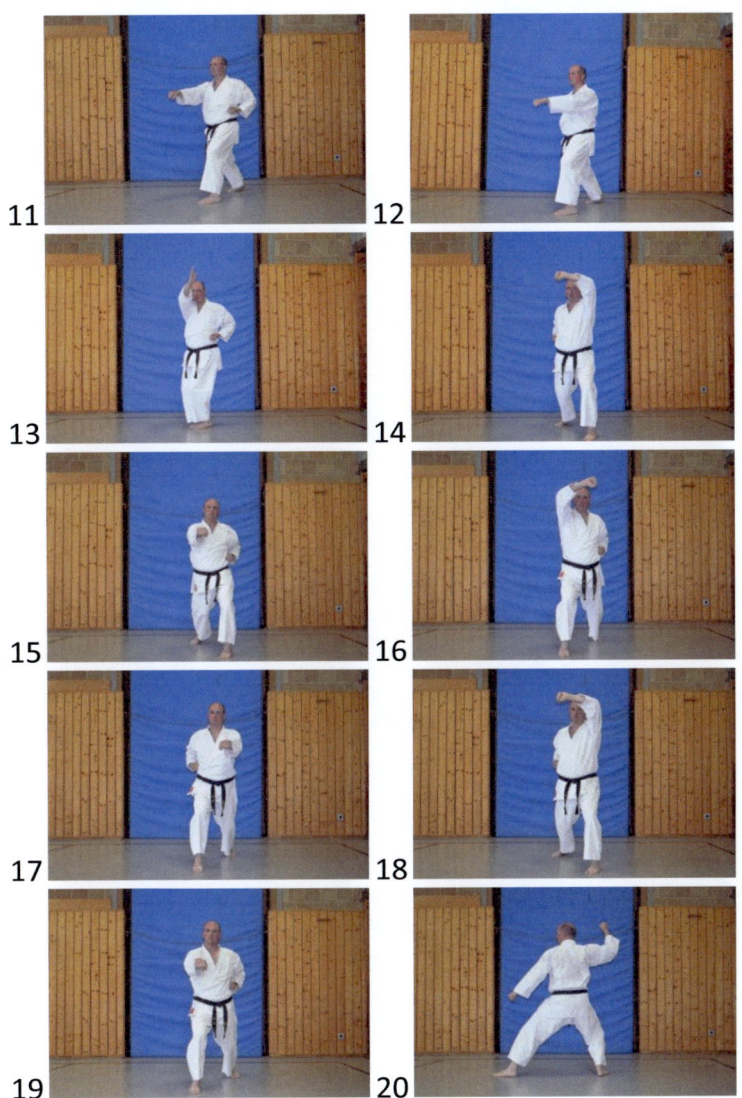

11   12

13   14

15   16

17   18

19   20

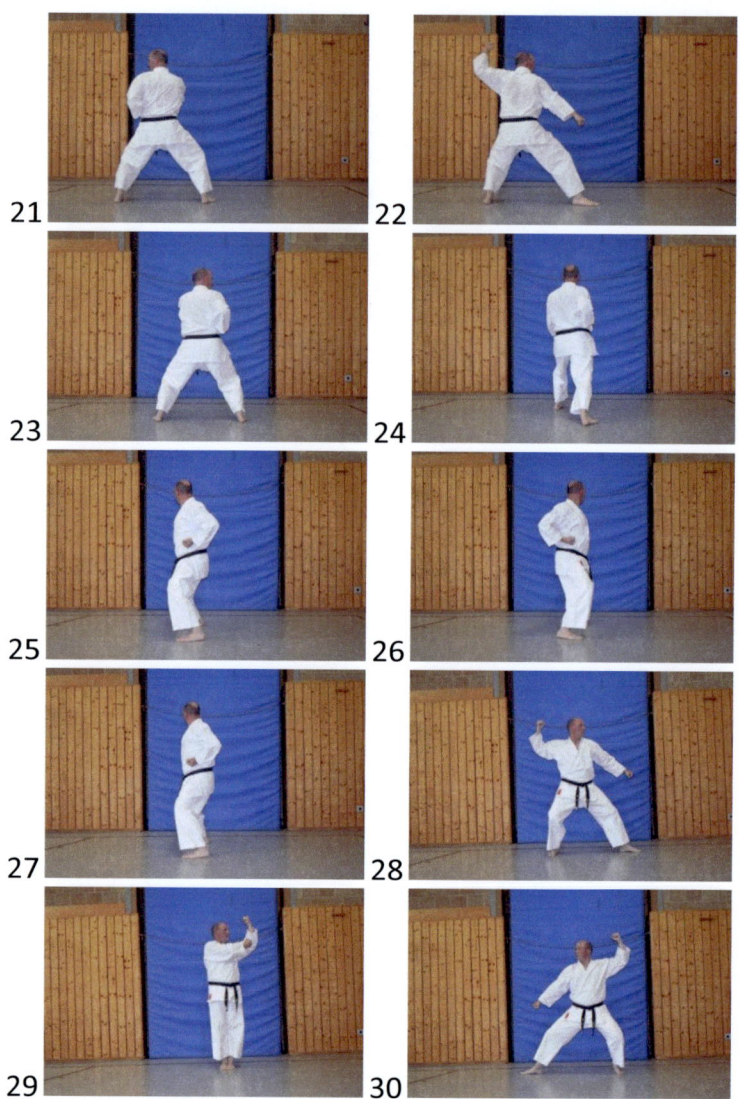

21 22

23 24

25 26

27 28

29 30

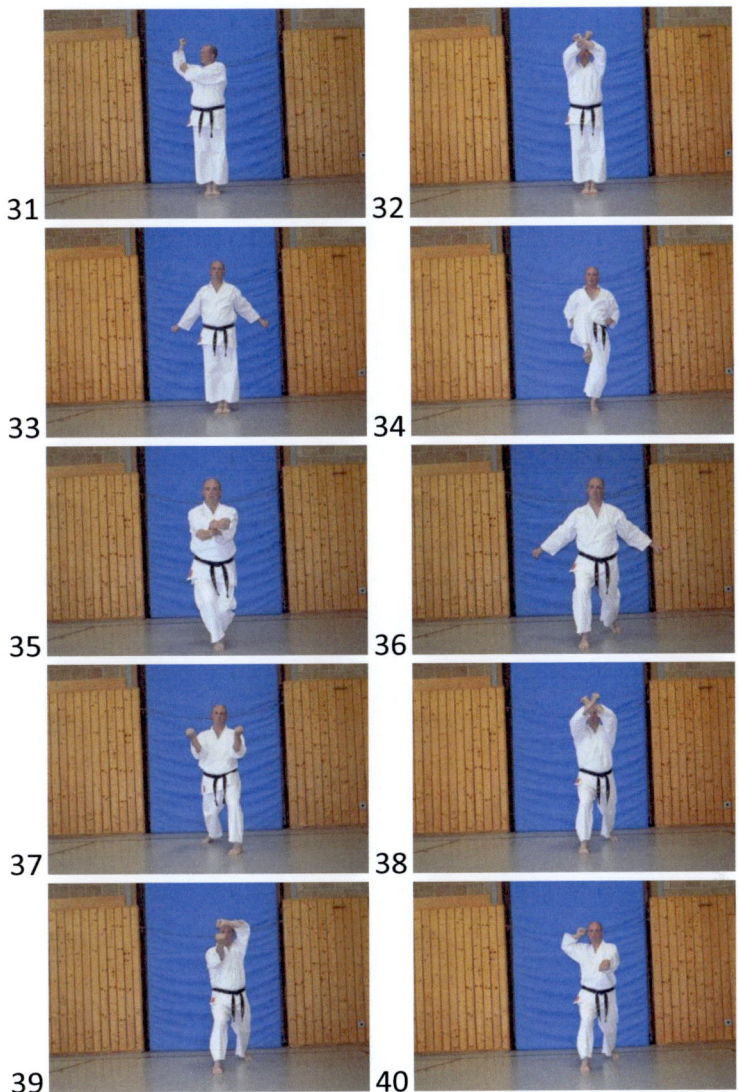

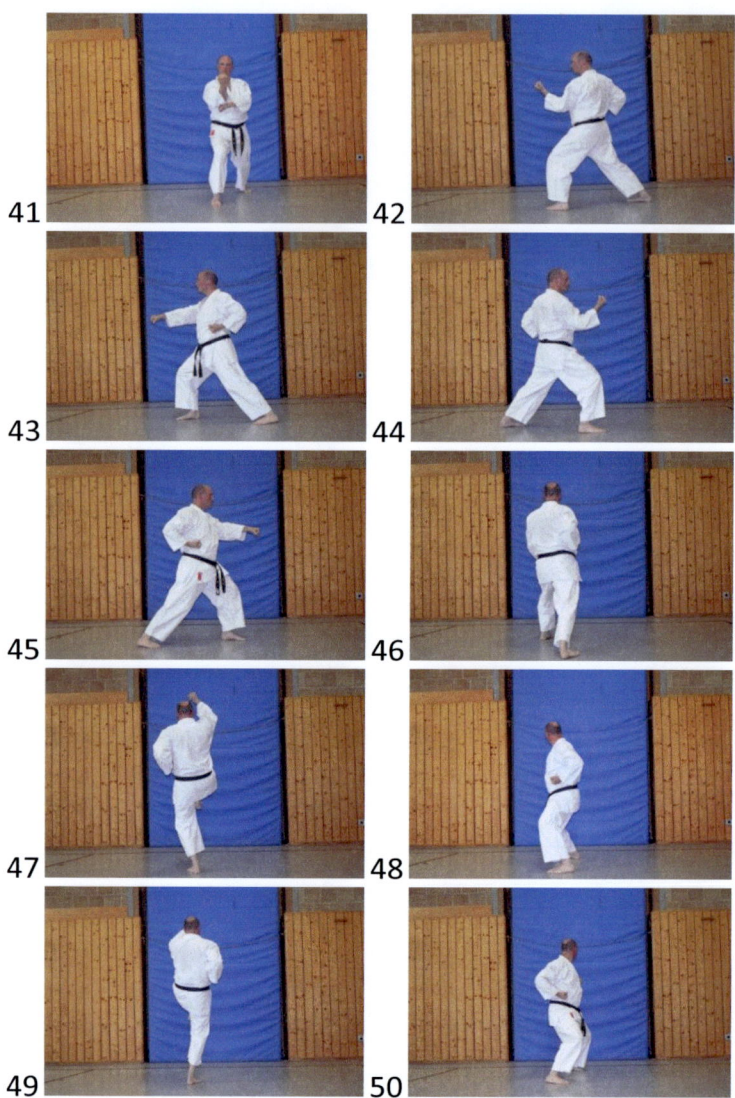

41　　　　　　　　42

43　　　　　　　　44

45　　　　　　　　46

47　　　　　　　　48

49　　　　　　　　50

51 52
53 54
55

Appendix 2: Jiin Form

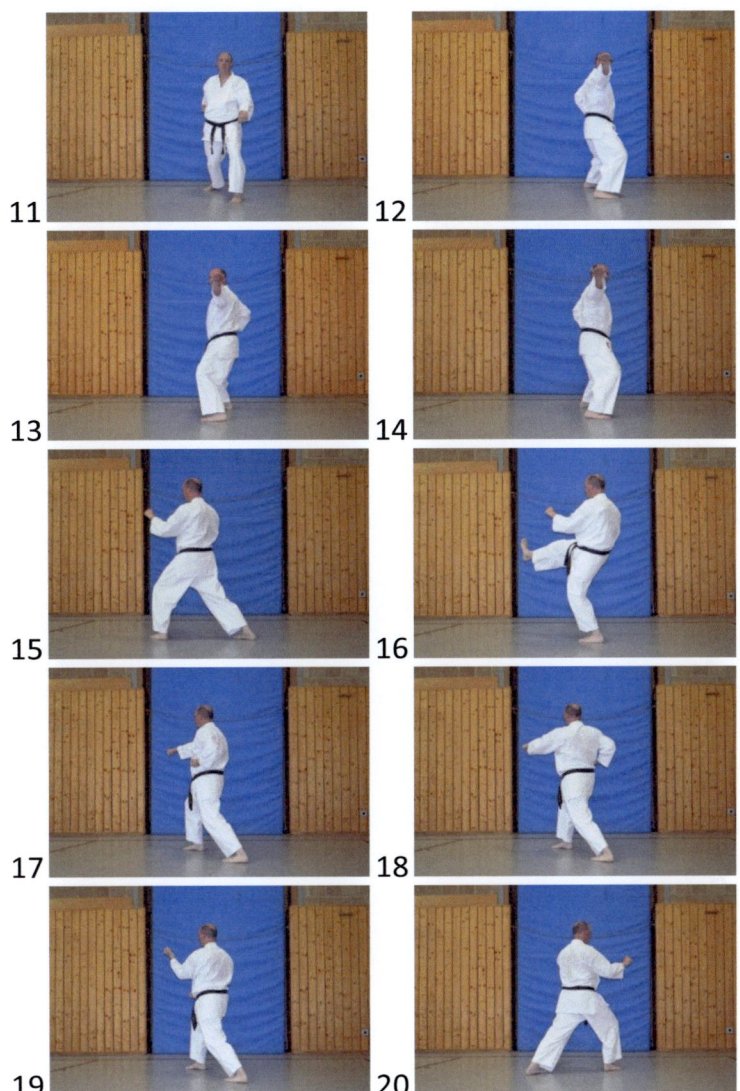

11   12

13   14

15   16

17   18

19   20

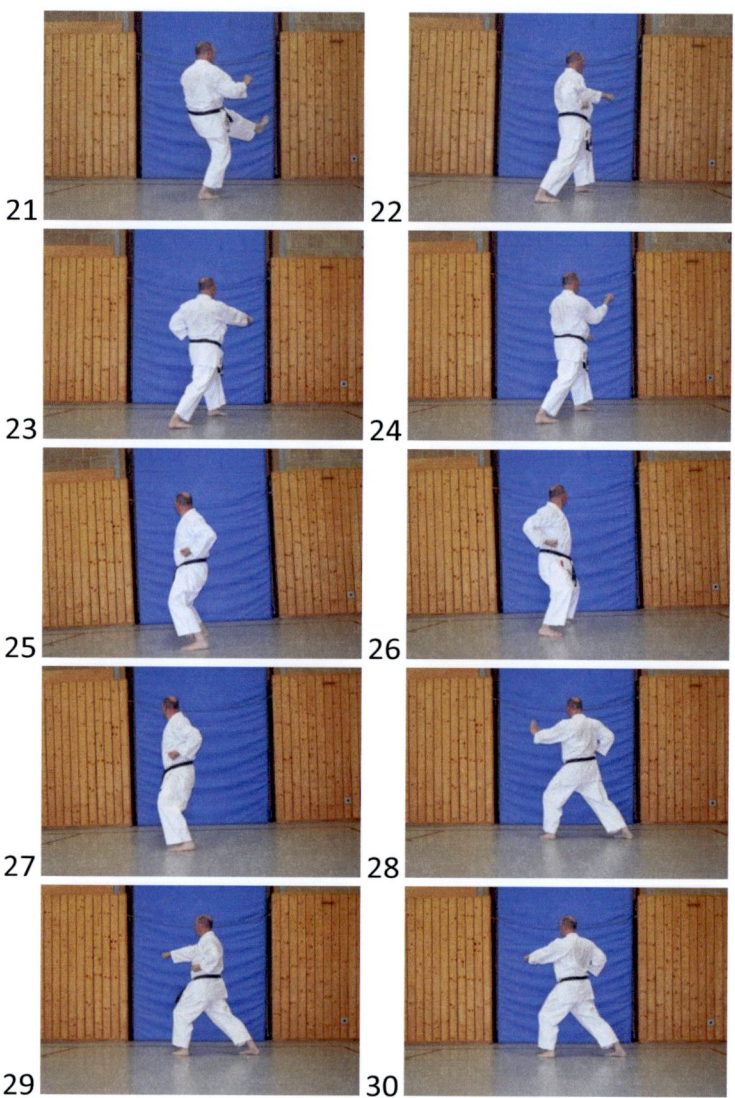

21 22

23 24

25 26

27 28

29 30

31

32

33

34

35

36

37

38

39

Appendix 3: Training Drill

This drill does not simulate reality. But it is an example how to train shifting between different techniques and to develop automatisms with a partner. A drill can consist of a single or a variety of moves. The complexity increases by adding techniques. If they are from a kata you don't necessarily need to put them in the order of the kata. The beauty of such a drill is that you can vary the order or even the techniques. In this case you explore the principles of the kata and train to make use of it. A drill can be designed in a way that at the end it flows automatically into a repetition either by changing the role of the attacker and defender or by letting one repeating the drill and changing roles later. Starting slowly at learning speed and power a drill should get faster and more powerful when repeating. This will help to increase the confidence in the application of the moves and enhance doing them without thinking.

The following pictures show the moves from the front for illustration reasons. They are not necessarily in the direction as they appear in the drill. The reader needs to test directions to see how the moves work best.

1) The drill starts with the opponent grabbing the neck and the throat.

Neck grab and choke (roles changed)

2) The defender disengages from the grip by hitting the choking elbow and pushing the arm down while pushing the other arm up with Age Uke.

Hit the elbow and push the arm down, push the other arm up

3) Moving behind the attacker by bringing the arm up (Kakiwake Uke)

Kakiwake Uke to bring arm over head

4) Try to apply arm lock with Gedan Barai, but opponent avoids it by moving around in other direction and grabbing the colar

5) The defender hits the elbow of the holding arm.

6) The same arm hits the head with an Uchi Uke backhand strike to the forward coming head.

7) Control holding arm with Uchi Uke arm and punch Oi Zuki with the other arm.

8) Opponent seizes colar with two hands and the defender counters with down block and Ura Zuki hook punch

9) The opponent launches a swing punch to the head. The defender hits the shoulder or breast while protecting the head from the side.

10) Kakiwake Uke like at the beginning to bring the arms over the head and come behind the opponent. Hit the head of the opponent with Mae Te Zuki.

11) Finish with a throw. Get the lead leg behind the opponent
    and push him back with the punching arm that he falls over
    the leg.

Opponent to get up again and start the drill from the beginning
either with or without changing roles.

Appendix 4: Bibliography

Abernethy, Iain: Bunkai Jutsu: The Practical Application of Karate Kata, UK: NETH Publishing, Cockermouth, 2002

Abernethy, Iain: Karate's Grappling Methods, UK: NETH Publishing, Cockermouth, 2000

Abernethy, Iain: Throws for Strikers: The Forgotten Throws of Karate, Boxing and Taekwondo, UK: NETH Publishing, Cockermouth, 2003

Braun, Christian: Grappling, Effektive Bodentechniken, GER: Meyer & Meyer Verlag, Aachen, 2005

Kane, Lawrence A. & Wilder, Kris: The Way of Kata: A Comprehensive Guide to Deciphering Martial Applications, USA: YMAA Publication Center, Boston, Mass., 2005

Patel, Rakesh: Practical Bunkai for the Shotokan Kata Jion, UK: E-Book, 2008

Pflüger, Albrecht: 27 Shotokan Katas, GER: FALKEN Verlag, Niedernhausen, 2001

Tartaglia, Fiore: Shotokan Kata bis zum Schwarzgurt, GER: SPECTRA Design & Fotografie, Göppingen, 2000

Tartaglia, Fiore: Shotokan Kata ab Schwarzgurt, GER: SPECTRA Design & Fotografie, Göppingen, 2002

Thompson, Geoff: Ground Fighting: The Escapes, Summersdale, Chichester, 1996